LEONARDO
DA VINCI

First paperback printing 2008
First published in North America in 2006 by the
National Geographic Society
1145 17th Street N.W.
Washington, D.C. 20036-4688

Copyright © 2006 Marshall Editions
A Marshall Edition
Conceived, edited, and designed by Marshall Editions
The Old Brewery, 6 Blundell Street, London N7 9BH, U.K.
www.quarto.com

Paperback ISBN: 978-1-4263-0248-0
Trade ISBN: 0-7922-5385-X
Library ISBN: 0-7922-5386-8

Originated in Hong Kong by Modern Age
Printed and bound in China by Midas Printing Limited

Publisher: Richard Green
Commissioning editor: Claudia Martin
Art director: Ivo Marloh
Picture manager: Veneta Bullen
Production: Anna Pauletti

Consultant: Dr. Gabriele Neher
Design and editorial: Tall Tree Ltd.

For the National Geographic Society:
Art director: Jim Hiscott
Project editor: Priyanka Lamichhane

One of the world's largest nonprofit scientific and educational organizations, the National Geographic Society was founded in 1888 "for the increase and diffusion of geographic knowledge." Fulfilling this mission, the Society educates and inspires millions every day through its magazines, books, television programs, videos, maps and atlases, research grants, the National Geographic Bee, teacher workshops, and innovative classroom materials. The Society is supported through membership dues, charitable gifts, and income from the sale of its educational products. This support is vital to National Geographic's mission to increase global understanding and promote conservation of our planet through exploration, research, and education.

For more information, please call 1-800-NGS LINE (647-5463) or write to the following address:

NATIONAL GEOGRAPHIC SOCIETY
1145 17th Street N.W.
Washington, D.C. 20036-4688 U.S.A.

For information about bulk purchases, please contact National Geographic Books Special Sales at ngspecsales@ngs.org

Visit www.nationalgeographic.com/books

Previous page: Leonardo's most famous painting, the "Mona Lisa."
Opposite: A painting of St. John the Baptist, which Leonardo finished in around 1515.

LEONARDO
DA VINCI

THE GENIUS WHO DEFINED THE RENAISSANCE

JOHN PHILLIPS

NATIONAL GEOGRAPHIC

WASHINGTON, D.C.

CONTENTS

EARLY YEARS

STARTING WORK

A BUSY MAN

NEW CHALLENGES

EARLY YEARS

The Boy from Vinci

Leonardo da Vinci was trained as an artist, but in his long life he painted very few pictures, and many of those were never finished. Despite this, one of them, the "Mona Lisa," is now the most famous painting in the world. Leonardo had other interests besides art, such as mathematics and engineering. Today, Leonardo is thought of as an all-around genius.

Previous page: Leonardo sketched this landscape in 1473. Because he drew what he saw—unlike previous artists, who drew from their imaginations—this sketch has been described as the first true landscape drawing in Western art.

Below: The house in the village of Vinci, where Leonardo is said to have been born.

Leonardo was born in a remote village in Italy more than 550 years ago. The facts of his birth are known in surprising detail. This is thanks to his grandfather Antonio da Vinci who wrote about the birth in an old notebook. He had not written in his book for 16 years, and there was just enough space for him to squeeze one final entry onto the last page.

It is Antonio's neatly written note that records for history the birth of Leonardo. He was born in the village of Vinci on Saturday, April 15, 1452, at "the third hour of the night." This was the third hour after sunset, which is about 10:30 p.m. Antonio tells us that Leonardo was baptized the next day, and that five men and five women witnessed the ceremony.

1450

In Italy, the city-states of Florence, Naples, and Milan form an alliance.

1450

Francesco Sforza becomes the duke of Milan.

What's in a name?

Strangers would have known that Leonardo's father worked as a lawyer because he used the title "Ser" before his name. Lawyers were highly respected members of society, and the proper way to address them was by using this polite title.

Antonio noted that Leonardo was born to his son Ser Piero, who was a successful lawyer. But there is one thing Antonio does not give away: He does not say who Leonardo's mother was. Of course Antonio knew her identity, but he thought he had good reason to keep her name secret. Leonardo's parents were not married, and that made him an illegitimate child, which was then considered to be an embarrassment.

Little is known about Leonardo's mother. Historians tell us she was called Caterina and came from a poor family; she may have been a servant. She was in her mid-20s when she gave birth. There could be no future for Caterina and Ser Piero as a couple. They came from different social classes, and Ser Piero could not marry beneath him.

Below: The village of Vinci, where the da Vinci family had lived since the 13th century.

April 15, 1452
Leonardo da Vinci is born. He is the illegitimate son of Ser Piero da Vinci, a lawyer, and Caterina, a peasant woman.

1452
Leonardo's father marries Albiera Amadori. She becomes Leonardo's stepmother.

The village of Vinci lies in a region of central Italy called Tuscany. Leonardo's family had lived there for at least 200 years before his birth. They had taken the village name as their family name, which was common practice in Italy at that time. Several generations of da Vinci men had worked as lawyers and had made names for themselves in the nearby city of Florence. The family owned land and property in the village, and they were comfortable, but not wealthy.

Even though his father was a lawyer, Leonardo could never enter the family profession. Only the sons of married couples could become lawyers. This was the rule enforced by the guild, or company, of lawyers. All lawyers who worked in Florence were members of this guild.

Left: Vinci was a farming village where olives and grapes were grown. This picture shows the grape harvest in an Italian village, at about the time Leonardo was a boy.

1452
Lorenzo Ghiberti completes his bronze "Gates of Paradise" doors for Florence Cathedral.

1452–53
Leonardo lives with his mother, Caterina.

His earliest memory

In later life, Leonardo said he remembered an incident from when he was a baby. He said a kite (a kind of hawk with long tail feathers) flew down to his bed and flicked its tail against his lips. He wondered if this was the cause of his lifelong fascination with flight.

A few months after Leonardo was born, Ser Piero and Caterina went their separate ways. Ser Piero married Albiera Amadori, a girl from a rich family in Florence. He was in his mid-20s and ambitious. No doubt he had great plans for his career as a lawyer, and a "good marriage" would help his prospects. Although he did not take an active role in his baby son's life, he did not abandon the infant Leonardo. He may have helped to plan his baby's upbringing.

Leonardo spent the first year of his life with his mother, Caterina. He was then handed over to Ser Piero's parents, Antonio and Lucia da Vinci, possibly because the family felt they were more financially capable of taking care of him than his mother, and Ser Piero was busy in Florence. Antonio was in his 80s; Lucia, in her 60s. One of the couple's own children still lived at home, a teenager named Francesco. He worked on the family's land.

Shortly after Caterina handed Leonardo over to the da Vinci family, she married a local man, and they moved a short distance away from Vinci. They had five children, who were Leonardo's halfsisters and halfbrother. Even though Leonardo lived in his grandparents' house, he probably saw his mother and her other children when she came to Vinci for festivals. He may have seen his father less often, as Ser Piero's work kept him in Florence for much of the time. Some historians believe that Leonardo's unsettled childhood may have affected his personality, making him withdraw into his own imagination.

1453
Leonardo goes to live with his grandparents Antonio and Lucia da Vinci.

1455
The building of the Palazzo Venezia is completed in Rome. It is the ideal Renaissance palace.

Early Lessons

Above: In the 15th century, schools such as this one were only for the sons of wealthy families. Girls and poorer boys helped their parents or learned a trade.

Many historians have tried to unravel Leonardo's childhood, but there is still a great deal we do not know about his early years. However, we do know he was taught reading, writing, math, and music.

No doubt Leonardo knew and played with children his own age, but we know nothing about them. He might have played ball games, like bowling and a sort of football (soccer), and amused himself with simple toys like spinning tops and hoops. We do know that he formed an attachment to his uncle Francesco, who tended the olive groves, vineyards, and wheat fields owned by the family. Leonardo began to pick up the basic skills of farming from Francesco. It was at this time that Leonardo developed a fascination with nature that was to last throughout his life.

In the 15th century, most Italian children did not go to school. Wealthier boys went to grammar schools and learned to read and write Latin, but there is no evidence that Leonardo did. Years later, Leonardo described himself as an "unlettered man," by which he meant he had not been taught Latin.

1456
Filippo Brunelleschi dies. He was one of the first people to use perspective in art.

1464
Leonardo's first stepmother, Albiera, dies.

His first biographer

The first person to write a biography of Leonardo was Giorgio Vasari (1511–74). He never met Leonardo, but he spoke to people who had known him. Vasari's biography, published in 1550, might only be ten pages long (it's a chapter in a book about the lives of famous artists), but it contains useful information not found anywhere else.

Latin was the language of the ancient Romans. In Leonardo's day, it was still the language of lawyers, doctors, bankers, and the Christian church. Maybe he missed out on a full education because, as the son of unmarried parents, he would never be able to enter one of these professions. Because he was an illegitimate child, he was also prohibited from going to college. With his interest in nature, perhaps the da Vinci family expected him to become a farmer.

However, Leonardo was taught to read and write in Italian, probably by his family. He was left-handed, which at the time was considered a bad habit, but it seems that he was not forced to use his right hand—which could have been disastrous for his writing and drawing. Giorgio Vasari, who wrote an account of Leonardo's life, tells us that he was also taught arithmetic and music, and that he learned to play the lyre (a stringed instrument). Some historians believe that Leonardo's lack of a formal education helped to create an independent, free-thinking person.

> *"[Leonardo] would have been very proficient at his early lessons if he had not been so volatile and unstable; for he was always setting himself to learn many things only to abandon them almost immediately."*
> Giorgio Vasari, *Lives of the Artists*, 1550

1465
Leonardo's father marries Francesca di Ser Giuliano Lanfredini. She becomes Leonardo's second stepmother.

1465
Leonardo's grandfather dies.

The Changing Face of Portrait Painting

Leonardo da Vinci lived during a period we now call the Renaissance, from a French word meaning "rebirth." During the Renaissance, artists began to look more closely at the cultures of ancient Greece and Rome. They were inspired by the skill and realism of ancient art, and began to change the way they worked.

During the Middle Ages, artists did not paint portraits as we know them today. When they painted people, they showed them as characters from the Bible or from history and made up their features and dress from their imagination. Artists were not interested in painting the likeness of one individual, capturing them as they really were. All this changed in the Renaissance, when artists began to want to show the world as it really was, and to test their skill with new subjects. In the 1430s artists like Antonio Pisanello started to paint portraits of wealthy people.

Title: "Portrait of a Princess of the House of Este"
Artist: Antonio Pisanello
Date: 1436–38
This early Renaissance portrait shows the lady in profile, in the same way that ancient Greek and Roman artists had shown their subjects.

Title: "Portrait of Federico da Montefeltro"
Artist: Piero della Francesca
Date: 1472–74
This portrait shows Federico da Montefeltro, a duke from central Italy. The duke paid Piero della Francesca to record his likeness, just as he really was. The artist even painted the gap where the bridge of the duke's nose should be—it had been cut off by a sword blow. Piero has also given a sense of the duke's power in the stern expression on his face.

Title: "Portrait of a Young Man"
Artist: Sandro Botticelli
Date: c.1480
The name of this man, who probably came from Florence, is unknown. He is young, handsome, and looks confident. But most importantly, he is shown face-on rather than in profile. Botticelli, the artist, was one of the first Renaissance artists to paint people in this direct and dramatic way.

Title: "Cecilia Gallerani"
Artist: Leonardo da Vinci
Date: c.1490
Leonardo was a groundbreaking portrait painter and one of the greatest of the Renaissance. This portrait of Cecilia Gallerani was one of the first three-quarter portraits, where the sitter's body faces one way and her head twists the other. It is as if she were reacting to someone's calling her. Even her pet ermine (weasel) is distracted—as if a fleeting moment in time has been captured.

Moving to Florence

Florence was a wealthy and important city, 20 miles (32 km) from Vinci. In the second half of the 15th century, new buildings, roads, and public squares turned it into a beautiful city. Its wealthy citizens lived in splendid houses, which they grandly called palaces.

The da Vinci family had been connected with Florence for many years. It was where Ser Piero lived and worked as a lawyer. In the mid-1460s Leonardo joined him there. Several events happened at this time, some or all of which led to Ser Piero taking charge of Leonardo for the first time since his birth.

Ser Piero had a new job working as a lawyer for the Medici family, the most powerful people in Florence. His first wife, Albiera, died and he married a woman named Francesca. His parents died, and his brother Francesco got married. Ser Piero was now head of the family; he was in a good financial position; and there was no one left in Vinci to look after Leonardo. For a boy raised in the quiet of the country, a move to the big city must have been exciting.

Right: About 100,000 people lived in Florence in the 1460s. It was surrounded by walls and watchtowers, and the Arno River flowed through the center.

1466
Leonardo becomes a pupil of the artist Andrea del Verrocchio, in Florence.

1466
Verrocchio casts his bronze statue of the Biblical figure David.

Leonardo's master

Andrea del Verrocchio (1435–88) was busy and successful. He trained many young men to become artists. By the 1460s he was considered the best artist in Florence and was the official sculptor for the Medici family. He ran a large workshop that produced all manner of works of art for wealthy citizens, churches, and monasteries.

Right: This bronze figure of the Bible's David, with the head of the giant Goliath at his feet, was made by Verrocchio around 1466. Some people think Leonardo, about 14, was the model. It was common for apprentices to act as models.

The move to Florence was a turning point in Leonardo's life. Ser Piero had good contacts there, one of whom was a successful artist named Andrea del Verrocchio. He ran a workshop where he trained apprentices as painters and sculptors. Ser Piero knew Leonardo had a talent for drawing, and he arranged for him to become one of Verrocchio's pupils.

Verrocchio's workshop was a short walk from Ser Piero's office. Leonardo was 14 or 15 when he walked through its doors for the first time, into a large open space on the ground floor of a city-center building. It was a shop, called a *bottega*, just like that of a shoemaker, a butcher, or a tailor. Verrocchio's studio was like a small factory, producing works of art, including paintings for churches and portraits of the rich and famous, as well as suits of armor, theatrical costumes, and tombstones. It also had chickens, whose eggs were needed for food and for the work of the artists.

1469
Lorenzo de' Medici, of the powerful Medici family, comes to power in the republic of Florence.

1470
Leonardo paints a dog, a fish, and a boy's curly hair in Verrocchio's "Tobias and the Angel."

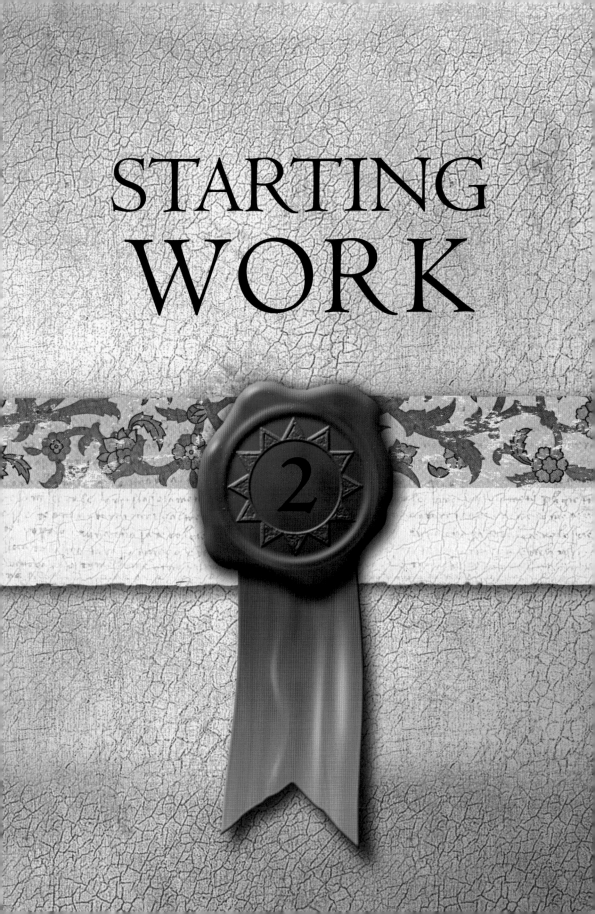

STARTING
WORK

2

Training to Be an Artist

An artist's apprentice usually spent about six years studying with his master. He began in the lowest grade, as the most junior person in the workshop, and gradually moved up to more responsible positions. After the apprentice had completed his training, he could become a master himself.

Leonardo and the other pupils lived with Verrocchio in rooms upstairs or at the back of his workshop. The apprentices' families paid Verrocchio for the boys' food and lodging. In return, Verrocchio taught them all he knew. Leonardo was not like the other apprentices. They were the sons of tradesmen—butchers, leatherworkers, bakers—sent to learn a practical trade. Leonardo was the son of a wealthy professional man, prevented from learning his father's work because of his illegitimate birth. He was also quite old to start as an apprentice. Most boys started at about 12 years or younger.

Left: "Tobias and the Angel" was painted in Verrocchio's workshop circa 1470. It is thought that Leonardo painted the white dog at the angel's feet, the fish held by Tobias, and even the boy's curly hair.

Previous page: A detail from "The Annunciation," painted by Leonardo circa 1473. It shows the angel Gabriel kneeling down to tell the Virgin Mary that she is to have a child.

1472
Leonardo finishes his training with Verrocchio and becomes a member of the painters' guild of Florence.

1473
Leonardo's stepmother, Francesca, dies.

Nature's paintbox

Artists mixed their colors from natural materials. The browns and yellows of ocher and umber came from minerals, black from plants, white from lead and tin, the finest blue from lapis lazuli (a semiprecious stone), green from the mineral malachite, and red from the mineral cinnabar.

To the other pupils he may have seemed like the odd one out, but his personal circumstances did not affect his progress, and Leonardo quickly became Verrocchio's star pupil.

An artist's workshop had a strict way of working. At first, Leonardo would simply have observed Verrocchio at work, listening as he explained his methods, running errands, and tidying up for him. In time, he would have learned to make brushes and prepare paints. Only when Verrocchio believed that Leonardo was ready would he have taught his pupil how to draw. Leonardo would have practiced drawing the human figure and landscapes. From here, Leonardo would have moved on to copying his master's drawings onto wooden panels and walls, ready to be colored in.

Verrocchio also taught Leonardo how to work with stone, clay, wood, and metal. As he progressed, Leonardo was trusted to do more work for Verrocchio. His job, like that of the other pupils, was to do the groundwork for a piece of art that, as master, Verrocchio finished off. It was teamwork, for which the workshop master took all the credit.

"To make a fine green take green and mix it with bitumen and you will make the shadows darker."

Leonardo da Vinci, *Notebooks*

August 5, 1473
Leonardo sketches his earliest surviving drawing, showing a landscape (see page 7).

1473
Leonardo paints an angel in Verrocchio's "Baptism of Christ."

In the final stage of his training, Leonardo was taught how to paint. He learned both panel painting (painting on flat pieces of wood) and fresco painting (painting onto plastered walls). Before an artist began to paint a fresco, an outline of the painting had to be transferred to the plaster. A full-size drawing, called a cartoon, was made on paper. The outline was pricked with holes, and the paper was fixed to the wall. Powdered charcoal was dusted over the drawing and, as it fell through the holes, it made a dotted version of the drawing on the plaster. It could then be colored in. For panels, the drawing could be made directly onto the wood.

Leonardo first learned a style of painting called *tempera*, in which ground-up powdered pigments (colors) were mixed with water and fresh egg yolk—that's why Verrocchio's workshop kept chickens. The egg yolk bound the pigments together. The problem with tempera was that it dried quickly, so artists had to work fast—something Leonardo found hard to do. Luckily for him, a new style of painting was becoming fashionable. This was oil painting, a technique that reached Italy from the Netherlands. Leonardo preferred painting in oils, so he could work at his own pace.

Right: This document records Leonardo's admission to the painters' guild of Florence in 1472. His name appears as "Lionardo D.S. (di Ser) Piero da Vinci" (Lionardo was another way of spelling his name). After this is the word *dipintore*, meaning "practicing painter."

1473

Leonardo completes his first painting entirely on his own, "The Annunciation."

1475

Leonardo's father marries Margherita di Francesco. She becomes Leonardo's third stepmother.

Right: Leonardo's first portrait was of Ginevra de' Benci. Ginevra was about 19 in 1476, when Leonardo painted her portrait on a wood panel. This beautiful painting is one of the few that Leonardo ever completed.

However, Leonardo was not yet free to paint his own pictures. He was still Verrocchio's pupil, and this meant adding details to Verrocchio's paintings, as he did with the painting "Tobias and the Angel" (see page 20). But in the summer of 1472, at the age of 20, Leonardo completed his training with Verrocchio and became a member of the painters' guild of Florence. Leonardo could now work for himself. However, he did not set up his own workshop right away. Instead, he chose to stay in Verrocchio's workshop as an assistant. In 1473 he completed his first painting entirely on his own, "The Annunciation" (see page 19).

There is a famous story from this period in Leonardo's life, as told by his first biographer, Giorgio Vasari. He said that Leonardo added an angel to one of Verrocchio's paintings ("Baptism of Christ," c. 1473). Vasari tells us that, because Verrocchio thought the angel was so much better than anything he could paint, he never painted again. But Vasari was no doubt flattering Leonardo, and the story may not be entirely true.

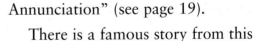

Club for artists

Many artists in Florence belonged to the city's painters' guild, the Compagnia di San Luca (the Company of St. Luke). Artists had to join the guild if they wanted to open their own workshops in the city. St. Luke is the patron saint of artists because, according to legend, he was a painter himself and may have painted portraits of Jesus and Mary.

1475
Michelangelo Buonarroti, who will become one of the world's greatest painters, is born near Florence.

February 26, 1476
Leonardo's first stepbrother, Antonio, is born.

Struggling to Make a Living

Leonardo worked as Verrocchio's assistant for about five more years until, around 1477, he set out on his own. He was about 25. It must have taken courage for him to leave the security of an employer who gave him work, board, and lodging.

At first, Leonardo struggled to earn a living. Florence was a city of artists, competing against each other for work. In the 1470s there were at least 30 painters' workshops, all seeking work from the city's wealthy citizens and the church. Leonardo discovered that finding a patron (employer) was no easy task, but it was vital if he wanted to survive as an artist. Leonardo might have hoped to be patronized by Lorenzo de' Medici (1449–92), the head of the city's most powerful family, but Lorenzo gave all his commissions to other artists.

Leonardo faced personal difficulties, too. In 1475 his father, Ser Piero, had remarried, following the death of his second wife, Francesca.

Left: Leonardo would have been inspired by altarpieces such as this, painted by Fra Angelico around 1440 for a church in Florence. It shows Christ being taken down from the Cross. It is painted on a panel of wood and has a gilded frame.

1476
Leonardo paints a portrait of Ginevra de' Benci (see page 23).

1477
Leonardo sets up his own workshop in Florence.

Altarpieces

An altarpiece was an important religious painting designed to fit behind a church altar. The largest churches had several altarpieces, painted by leading artists of the day. At a time when most people could not read, paintings in churches were vital for telling Bible stories.

In 1476, his new wife, Margherita, had borne him a son, named Antonio. This boy was Ser Piero's first legitimate child. Because Antonio was a "proper" son, not only could he follow Ser Piero into a legal career but he could also inherit his wealth. Perhaps it was this that spurred Leonardo to work for himself, knowing that he would always have to earn his own living.

January 10, 1478, was a big day for Leonardo. His workshop received its first commission for a painting. He was asked to paint an altarpiece showing the Nativity, or birth of Jesus, for the Chapel of San Bernardo in Florence. He took on an apprentice, a teenager named Paolo da Firenze. Despite being paid in advance for the painting, Leonardo never finished it. Maybe he lost interest or was unhappy with the quality of his work. Whatever the reason, this reveals an important side of Leonardo's character: time and again throughout his life, he left work unfinished. In 1480 he started a picture of St. Jerome but never completed it. However, what Leonardo did paint was remarkable, and people began to take note of him as an artist.

Right: Leonardo's painting of St. Jerome was begun about 1480, but never finished. The painting shows the saint with a lion. Wealthy families in Florence owned wild animals, so Leonardo had probably seen a real lion to draw from.

1478

Leonardo is commissioned to paint an altarpiece for the Chapel of San Bernardo, in Florence.

1478

Sandro Botticelli completes "Primavera" (Spring), one of the greatest paintings of the Renaissance.

Finding a Patron

A patron was a person or an institution that paid an artist to create a work of art. The system of patronage reached a high point in Renaissance Italy. The country's leading families, such as the Medici family of Florence, had grown rich through banking and trade. They saw it as their duty to commission artists to create great works of art for churches to educate people about Christianity. They also wanted beautiful sculptures and paintings for their own palaces. An artist relied entirely on his patrons for work and money, so it was his patrons who decided on his subjects and even influenced his manner of working. Leonardo had many patrons during his career. There were times when he got on well with a patron, but at other times he found the system frustrating.

Below: In 1460 the artist Benozzo Gozzoli was instructed by the Medici to paint the walls of their private chapel, and this is one of the results, the "Procession of the Magi." It shows a young king (one of the magi who visited the baby Jesus) at the head of a procession. The four men on horseback are actually portraits of members of the Medici family. By having themselves portrayed in the picture, the Medici were showing off their financial and political power to all who saw it.

Right: In August 1502 Leonardo had a new patron. He was appointed military engineer to the powerful Cesare Borgia, whose armies were fighting for control of central Italy. Borgia issued Leonardo with this passport, which granted him permission to travel freely throughout his territories and inspect his fortifications.

Left: In the 15th century, Italy was not a united country as it is today. Instead, the region was divided up into several states, each ruled from a major city. The Medici family ruled the region of Florence. Other powerful families (and possible patrons) included the d'Este in Ferrara, and the Sforza family in Milan.

SAVOY

MILAN

Milan

SALUZZO

MONTFERRAT

GENOA

MODENA

MANTUA

Mantua

FERRARA

LUCCA

Vinci

Pisa

Florence

FLORENCE

Imola

VENETIAN REPUBLIC

Venice

Adriatic Sea

SIENA

PAPAL STATES

Rome

KINGDOM OF NAPLES

Naples

Mediterranean Sea

SICILY

Leaving Florence

By 1481 Leonardo was ready for a change. In the four years since leaving the security of Verrocchio's workshop, he had struggled to make a living in Florence. He had failed to win the patronage of Lorenzo de' Medici, and work that he had taken on had been left unfinished.

Perhaps Leonardo's habit of not finishing his work earned him a reputation for being unreliable. Maybe his family background, his lack of education, and even his country accent singled him out as an "odd character," someone who did not fit in well with the artistic community in Florence. In October 1481, Pope Sixtus IV asked Lorenzo de' Medici to send the best Florentine artists to Rome to decorate the Sistine Chapel in the Vatican, the headquarters of the Christian church. Leonardo was not chosen.

However, Leonardo did have one talent that Lorenzo de' Medici recognized—music. Leonardo played the lyre and had a good singing voice.

Left: Early in 1481 the monks of San Donato monastery commissioned Leonardo to paint them an altarpiece, the "Adoration of the Magi." They gave him 30 months to paint it, but he broke the agreement. When he left Florence at the end of 1481, the painting was unfinished.

1480
Leonardo begins a painting of St. Jerome, but never finishes it.

1480
In Milan, Ludovico Sforza seizes power from his nephew.

It is said that Lorenzo de' Medici arranged for Leonardo to go to Milan, where he would work as a court musician. He was to be a "diplomatic gift" from Lorenzo to Ludovico Sforza, the duke of Milan. However, another version of this story says Leonardo was invited to Milan by Ludovico Sforza. Either way, Leonardo was ready to leave Florence.

At about this time he scribbled the word *dispero* on a page in one of his notebooks. It means "I despair." Historians interpret this in many ways. Some say it shows his frustration at being

Special friends

Although he was never interested in getting married or having children, Leonardo had many close friends and companions throughout his life. At the time he was leaving Florence, his closest friends were Fioravante di Domenico and Bernardo di Simone. Little is known about them other than that Leonardo wrote their names in a notebook alongside the word "friends."

overlooked by patrons. Others say it refers to the fact that he was feeling troubled and alone. Approaching 30, Leonardo was certainly at a crossroads in his life. In the autumn of 1481, he closed his workshop in Florence and prepared to leave for Milan. The city, and the glittering court of Ludovico Sforza, promised a new start.

Left: Peering out from the brown varnish on the right-hand edge of the "Adoration of the Magi" is a young man. Many people believe it is a self-portrait of Leonardo, at about 29.

1481
Leonardo is commissioned to paint the "Adoration of the Magi" for the San Donato monastery in Florence.

1481
Leonardo leaves Florence for Milan to work for Ludovico Sforza.

A BUSY
MAN

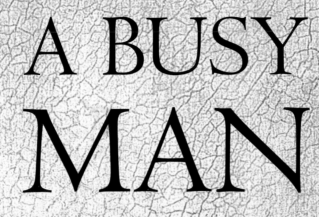

Arrival in Milan

Milan was 190 miles (305 km) north of Florence and was home to about 80,000 people. Leonardo had no intention of just working as a musician in Milan—the worlds of art, engineering, and theater all beckoned.

Among the items Leonardo took to Milan was a lyre, which he had made himself. It is said to have been made of silver shaped like a horse's head. Such an odd-looking instrument was bound to attract attention, which was possibly what Leonardo wanted. Maybe he hoped to use it to strike up a conversation with rich people and form a relationship which could lead to some work. Leonardo wrote a boastful letter in his notebook to Ludovico Sforza.

Left: One of Leonardo's many preparatory drawings for the Sforza Monument. It was to be in honor of Francesco Sforza, Ludovico's father. By the time Leonardo was ready to cast the statue, the bronze he would have used had been made into cannons. The cast itself was destroyed by French soldiers in 1499.

Previous page: Christ in Leonardo's "The Last Supper," which was painted on the wall of the monastery of Santa Maria delle Grazie, Milan, in 1495.

1483
Leonardo is commissioned to paint the "Virgin of the Rocks."

1486
Leonardo's stepmother, Margherita, dies.

The horse is built!

In 1999 a bronze horse was built to Leonardo's designs and given to the city of Milan by the United States. It weighed 15 tons and was 23 ft (7 m) tall—just as Leonardo had planned it. Another horse was cast from the same mold. Known as the "American Horse," it stands in the Frederik Meijer Gardens, Grand Rapids, Michigan.

He described what he could offer the duke, on top of playing the lyre. At the head of his list Leonardo claimed he had skills as a military engineer, saying he could build bridges, cannons, armored cars, and siege-machines. He put his skills as an artist at the bottom of the list. Leonardo guessed that the duke would be interested in war machines because Milan was under threat from other Italian city-states, as well as the French. No one knows if he ever sent the letter, but it paints a picture of Leonardo as a true "Renaissance man," with skills in a wide range of areas.

Leonardo had to wait eight years before Ludovico Sforza gave him a commission for a piece of art. Until then he busied himself with many different projects. He set up his own workshop to handle commissions such as a "Virgin of the Rocks" altarpiece, designed theater stage sets and costumes, and entered a competition, which he lost, to design a tower for Milan cathedral.

The project that Ludovico Sforza offered Leonardo, in 1489, was to create a bronze statue of a horse and rider. This was an important commission, and Leonardo hoped it would be a turning point. He was right—from then on, work would be much easier to come by. Sadly, the statue was never finished. In 1494 the forces of the French king Charles VIII invaded Italy. The bronze from which the statue would have been cast was sent away to be made into cannons to fight against the French.

1486

Leonardo's father marries Lucrezia di Guglielmo Cortigiani. She becomes Leonardo's fourth stepmother.

1487

Leonardo enters a competition to design a tower for Milan cathedral.

Friends and Apprentices

Leonardo the artist was also Leonardo the teacher. In the same way he had been taught the skills of an artist by his teacher, Andrea del Verrocchio, so Leonardo passed on his knowledge to his own apprentices. Several of them became close friends.

Leonardo had run a workshop in Florence before leaving the city. One of his apprentices there was a teenager named Paulo da Firenze. Paulo was skilled in the art of marquetry (using thin pieces of different colored woods to make pictures), which was highly fashionable at the time. However, according to one of Leonardo's letters, Paulo kept "bad company," and the apprentice was forced to leave Florence. He was at Leonardo's workshop for only a year.

Another apprentice was Tommaso di Giovanni Masini, known as Zoroastro. The son of a gardener, he joined Leonardo when he was about 16, working as his color-mixer at his workshop in Milan in the 1490s. Several other boys and young men are known to have worked at Leonardo's Milan workshop, one of whom deserves special mention.

"I went to supper... and the aforesaid Giacomo [Salai] ate for two, and did mischief for four, in so far as he broke three table flasks, and knocked over the wine."
Leonardo da Vinci, Notebooks

1488
Verrocchio, Leonardo's former teacher, dies.

1489
Ludovico Sforza commissions Leonardo to create a bronze statue of a horse and rider in honor of his father.

Leonardo wrote this in a notebook: "Giacomo came to live with me on the feast of St. Mary Magdalene [July 22] of the year 1490. He is ten years old." The boy's full name was Giovanni Giacomo di Pietro Caprotti, but he was better known by the nickname Salai (meaning "Little Devil" or "Imp"). Leonardo wrote more about Salai in his notebooks than about any other person.

Within months of moving in with Leonardo, Salai had stolen a pen from an apprentice and another a short while later. Leonardo was sure that Salai stole money from him and from other people. From Leonardo's notes a picture emerges of Salai as an unruly boy. Leonardo described him as a thief, a liar, obstinate, and greedy, but he

Above: On the right is a portrait of Salai in his late teens, drawn by Leonardo. He was a handsome young man with the face of an angel and ringlets of curly hair. The old bald man on the left may be Leonardo, as he thought he would look in old age.

warmed to him. Despite an age difference of some 28 years, Leonardo and Salai struck up a friendship that lasted almost 30 years. Salai became his closest friend and companion, and Leonardo may have thought of him as his adopted son. When Leonardo died, he remembered Salai in his will, leaving him a house and land in Milan, and probably some paintings, too. One of these paintings is believed to have been the "Mona Lisa," Leonardo's masterpiece.

1489
Leonardo starts his studies of human anatomy.

July 22, 1490
Leonardo takes in ten-year-old Giovanni Giacomo di Pietro Caprotti, known as Salai.

Leonardo's Notebooks

In the 1480s Leonardo began writing and sketching in notebooks. He carried them wherever he went, using them to record ideas as they occurred to him. Over the years he may have written and sketched as many as 20,000 pages, of which about 7,000 pages have survived. Even though we have less than half of what he wrote, the books give us a remarkable insight into how Leonardo worked and what he thought. Leonardo liked notebooks with wraparound covers made from leather or vellum (a fine type of paper made from calfskin). They were fastened with a small wooden toggle that passed through a loop of cord. Inside were pages of handmade paper, which he wrote on mainly in ink. There are pages of sketches, drafts of letters, comments on people and places, thoughts about art, the power of water, the workings of the human body, and much, much more.

Left: Leonardo made this detailed drawing of a horse's head and neck in one of his notebooks. It is thought to show his ideas for how he would cast the bronze for the Sforza Monument. The drawing shows the outer casing of the mold. Leonardo knew that until the molten bronze had cooled, it would put a great strain on the mold. He planned to reinforce the outside of the mold with metal rods, as shown in his drawing. They would help the statue keep its shape. When the bronze had set solid, the outer casing would be removed.

Above: A sketch of a building and Leonardo's description of it in "mirror writing." He could write from left to right, but it was easier for him to write backward because he was left-handed and it prevented his writing hand from smudging the text. It also made it harder for people to read the private things he wrote in his notebooks.

Right: This notebook is known as the Codex Leicester, after its 18th-century English owner, the Earl of Leicester. It is a collection of notes about physics, which Leonardo wrote c. 1507–10. It is now owned by Bill Gates, the cofounder of Microsoft, who bought it in 1994 for $30 million.

The Power of Water

Leonardo's notebooks contain many ideas that were well ahead of their time. In them he jotted down his original ideas on art, science, engineering, and human anatomy. Leonardo was also interested in the study of water.

Water fascinated Leonardo. He believed that "water is to the world as blood is to our bodies." His notebooks contain sketches of storms, whirlpools, waves, and drops of water, together with designs for inventions connected with water. He sketched how it might be possible to walk on water using floats. He also drew a man wearing a swim ring or life preserver: This simple device is familiar to swimmers today, but it was years ahead of its time when Leonardo sketched it.

Left: Leonardo designed many watercraft, including dredgers, paddle boats, and even submarines. In this design for a dredger he showed how silt—a fine sand that could choke up waterways—might be removed from canals, rivers, and harbors.

September 7, 1490
Salai steals a pen from one of Leonardo's assistants.

February 1491
Leonardo designs costumes for the wedding festivities of Ludovico Sforza and Beatrice d'Este of Ferrara.

Words for water

Leonardo listed 64 different words to describe the motions of water. His list begins: "Rebound, circulation, revolution, rotating, turning, repercussing, submerging, surging, declination, elevation, depression, consumation, percussion, destruction."

He dreamed of turning marshland into huge reservoirs, and he even planned to wash the streets of Milan clean using a system of locks and paddle wheels. One project occupied his thoughts for many years. This was the creation of a canal from the Arno River that would link Florence with the sea. He mapped its route many times but, like many of his big ideas, it came to nothing.

Historians have wondered why Leonardo was so interested in water. One answer is that, in an age before gasoline or electricity, the power of water could have many practical uses, and Leonardo made it his business to design machines that used it. Another answer is that his interest stemmed from his childhood, when two events made a lasting impression on him. When he was four years old, a great storm, as strong as a hurricane, had blown over the village of Vinci. When he was 14, the Arno River had burst its banks and flooded Florence. As an eyewitness to the destructive power of water, perhaps Leonardo had grown up in awe of it.

It's clear that Leonardo used his skills of observation to study water in all its forms. We call this a "scientific approach." His investigations took place before many scientists thought it necessary to make detailed observations and experiments to test their theories. Leonardo became confident in his ability to tame water, whether in a grand scheme such as a canal, or in clever devices designed to harness its incredible power.

1492
Lorenzo de' Medici, ruler of Florence and patron of the arts, dies.

1493
Leonardo's clay model for the Sforza Monument is put on display in Milan.

The Dream of Flight

Another study dominated the pages of Leonardo's notebooks during the 1490s: the mystery of flight. He watched birds flap their wings and glide effortlessly, high above the ground. He sketched them in his notebooks, asking himself, "How do birds fly?" His research into bird flight led to his designing machines intended to master the skies.

Leonardo believed the bird that came to him when he was a baby had been an omen that predicted his future interest in flight. In the same way that he used his powers of observation to study water, he applied his inquiring mind to understanding how birds took off, flew, and landed. He dissected (cut open) the wings of dead birds to study their bones and muscles.

From these studies, he hoped to design a device that could fly, thinking if birds could do it, then why not humans? His flying-machine would be a "ship of the air," and his notebooks contain sketches for several devices.

Above: Leonardo drew this device, which he called an "air screw." It worked on similar principles to the modern helicopter. He wrote, "I think, if this screw instrument is well made from linen and is turned rapidly, then said screw will climb upwards."

1494
Charles VIII of France invades Italy.

November 17, 1494
The bronze for the Sforza Monument is sent away to be made into cannons.

Right: A modern model of Leonardo's "air screw," built exactly to his design.

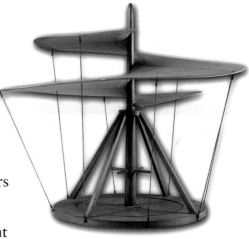

One of these designs was a pedal-powered wing, with a pilot suspended beneath it. As the person pedaled, the wing flapped. In another machine, the pilot stood upright and operated two pairs of wings that turned in circles.

By about 1495 Leonardo was confident enough to begin experimenting with some of his flying machines. Some people believe he actually built some of these devices. They think he made small models to test his ideas, and one device that was big enough to support an adult human—himself. In a notebook he describes how he planned to jump from the roof of a building in Milan using a device that was similar to a modern hang glider. However, he never took the risk. Leonardo noted that if he was to try out his machine, then he should do so over a lake with a life preserver around his waist, "so that if you fall in, you will not be drowned."

Leonardo was not the first person to wonder about flight, but he was the first known to make a serious scientific study of the possibilities. Once again, he was ahead of his time.

First parachute

Leonardo invented the parachute in around 1485. He sketched it in one of his notebooks, saying a person "could fall from any height without injury." His design was finally put to the test on June 26, 2000, when the English skydiver Adrian Nicholas jumped from an altitude of 10,000 ft (3,000 m). The pyramid-shaped parachute worked perfectly.

1495
Venice, Milan, Rome, and Spain form an alliance against the French, who have captured the city of Naples.

July 1495
The alliance of Italian city-states defeats the French at the Battle of Fornovo.

Fragile Fresco

By 1495 Leonardo had been in Milan for nearly 15 years, but he had little to show for it. He'd painted a portrait of Cecilia Gallerani (see page 15), Ludovico Sforza's girlfriend, but plans for his Sforza horse statue had come to a halt because of the French invasion. But his luck was due to change.

Below: Leonardo's "The Last Supper" is a masterpiece of perspective, creating the illusion of a three-dimensional room. The eyes are drawn straight to Christ at the center.

In 1495 the invading French forces were defeated in northern Italy by an alliance of Italian states. The time was right for Ludovico Sforza to turn his attention back to the arts. He commissioned Leonardo to paint "The Last Supper" on the wall of a dining room at the monastery of Santa Maria delle Grazie in Milan.

1495
Ludovico Sforza commissions Leonardo to paint "The Last Supper."

1498
Leonardo is commissioned to decorate several rooms in Castello Sforzesco, the home of the Sforza family.

Leonardo began by sketching ideas in his notebooks. From his rough drawings we can see how he thought carefully about composing the painting: where the figures should be, the arrangement of food on the table, the background, and how it would be seen from the ground—it is about 8 ft (2.4 m) off the floor. The painting shows the moment at which Christ has revealed that one of the apostles will betray him. Leonardo arranged the apostles in groups of three, showing them in shock as they talk about who the betrayer could be.

Christ's last meal

The Last Supper, as revealed in the Bible, is a key moment in Jesus Christ's life. It was the final meal he took with his disciples, on the night before his Crucifixion. This is the origin of the communion service, at which Christians share bread and wine (the body and blood of Christ) as Christ and his apostles had done.

According to legend, Leonardo was slow to complete the painting, even though he had assistants to help him. An eyewitness said he would go for days without making a brushstroke, but the same person also said he worked from dawn to dusk, never putting down his brush and forgetting to eat and drink! The truth is, Leonardo spent two to three years painting "The Last Supper," which was not very long considering the amount of work involved. He wasn't there every day, because he was busy with other projects in Milan, such as designing stage sets for a play.

The result was a masterpiece that has become one of Leonardo's most famous paintings. Unfortunately, soon after the picture was completed, the paint began to flake off. The fresco has been restored many times, and now only about 20 percent of what we see was actually painted by Leonardo—the rest is the work of many restorers, working to Leonardo's design.

1499
Milan is invaded by the French king Louis XII. Ludovico Sforza falls from power.

1499
Venice goes to war with the Ottoman Empire.

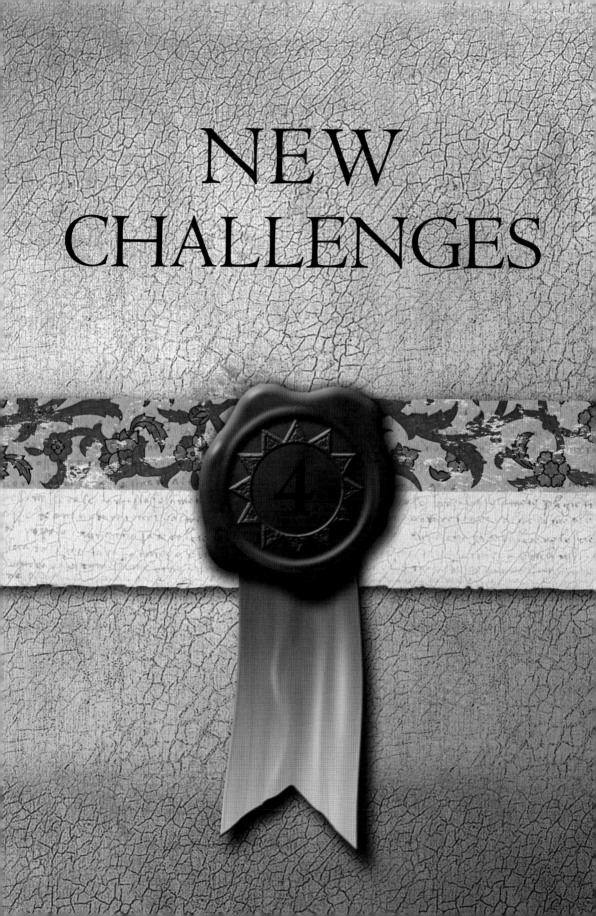

NEW CHALLENGES

Travels in Italy

Above: Leonardo made this map of Imola circa 1502. It is a detailed street-by-street plan, and is probably the first overhead map of a city. Most maps of the time were drawn at an angle and not from above.

Previous page: Leonardo sketched this portrait of himself when he was in his 60s. It shows him as an old man, with long, thin hair and a bushy beard.

It was the end of the 15th century, and the end of one chapter in Leonardo's life. At the age of 47, he was about to begin the next chapter, which included a period of new challenges, traveling, and other changes.

The peace that had returned to the city of Milan in 1495 was short-lived. In 1499 the city was invaded by the new French king, Louis XII. Ludovico Sforza was forced to flee, and Leonardo made plans to return to Florence. He transferred a large sum of money to a bank in Florence, packed his belongings into three cases, and left Milan in late December 1499 after almost 20 years in the city.

Accompanying Leonardo was Salai, who was now 19 and still living and working with him. Master and assistant did not go straight to Florence. Instead, they traveled southeast to the city of Mantua, where Leonardo made a drawing of Isabella d'Este, sister of Ludovico Sforza's wife. In early 1500 they reached Venice, where Leonardo came up with plans to flood a valley and destroy a Turkish army that was threatening the city. As with many of his ideas, the plan was never carried out.

December 1499
Leonardo leaves Milan for Mantua and Venice.

April 1500
Leonardo returns to Florence.

Right: One of Leonardo's cartoons for the "Virgin and Child with St. Anne," drawn around 1508. It measures 5 ft (1.5 m) tall and 3 ft (0.9 m) wide, and was drawn mainly in pencil on brown paper.

By April 1500 Leonardo was back in Florence. He met his elderly father, Ser Piero, his father's fourth wife, Lucrezia, and his 11 halfbrothers and halfsisters, who were between the ages of two and 24.

Leonardo had returned to Florence with no work to do. Once again, he was in need of a patron and somewhere to live. He took up lodgings with Salai in the Church of the Annunciation, whose monks commissioned him to paint them an altarpiece. It was to show the Virgin Mary, St. Anne, and the infants Jesus and John the Baptist. Over many years Leonardo made sketches and cartoons, but he never produced the painting. His attention had turned to mathematics, and he devoted much of his time to studying the subject. Perhaps it was this, together with his continuing travels, that stopped him from finishing the altarpiece. He visited Rome in 1501, and Imola, north of Florence, the following year. But he was always drawn back to Florence, where offers of new work awaited him.

Vegetarian

Leonardo was a vegetarian. He loved animals and would not let his body become what he called a "tomb for other animals." He believed that creatures capable of movement could feel pain, so he ate only what could not move—vegetables.

1501

Leonardo is commissioned to paint the "Virgin and Child with St. Anne" for the Church of the Annunciation.

1501

Leonardo visits Rome.

The Art of War

Leonardo lived in troubled times. He had witnessed the French invasion of Milan in 1499; he knew that Venice was at war with the Ottoman Empire; and he was well aware of conflicts between cities in Italy. As a result, many of his ideas had a military purpose.

From his earliest days in Milan in the 1480s, Leonardo had shown a keen interest in military engineering. His notebooks are filled with his thoughts about engineering matters, together with designs for new types of war machines. He gave a lot of thought to building defensive town walls. He also produced designs for bridges that could be taken down and put up elsewhere, escape tunnels, and secret underground rooms where people could hide. There are also designs for weapons, including a sword-eating shield, a giant catapult, a multibarrelled gun, a massive crossbow, a shrapnel-throwing cannon, and fire-throwers.

Left: A selection of war machines sketched by Leonardo on a page in a notebook. At the top is his design for a horse-powered vehicle with swirling knives, designed to cut through an enemy army. Below is his drawing for an armored car made from wood. It was never built, but Leonardo had designed an early tank.

1501
Leonardo paints "Madonna of the Yarnwinder."

August 1502
Leonardo is appointed military engineer to Cesare Borgia in Rome.

Right: A modern model of Leonardo's armored car. According to his notes, it needed eight men to operate it. Some turned cranks that moved its wheels; some kept lookout from the turret; and some fired cannons through the vehicle's portholes.

Leonardo had to wait more than 20 years before his military ambitions became reality. In August 1502 he was appointed engineer to the powerful Cesare Borgia (1475–1507), illegitimate son of Pope Alexander VI and commander of the pope's armies. Borgia planned to conquer the whole of Italy. He issued Leonardo with a passport that allowed him to travel freely (see page 27), and for six months the artist visited cities loyal to Borgia. Leonardo made suggestions for how their fortifications could be improved. Although he worked for Borgia for less than a year, it was a very productive time.

This interest in military work does not mean that Leonardo liked war. He just wanted to use his intelligence to help people in the troubled times in which they lived. "I never tire of being useful," he wrote in a notebook.

> "Also I will make covered cars, safe and unassailable, which will enter among the enemy with their artillery, and there is no company of men at arms so great that they will not break it. And behind these the infantry will be able to follow quite unharmed and without any hindrance."
> **Leonardo da Vinci, letter to Ludovico Sforza, c. 1481**

1502–3
Leonardo travels around Italy in Borgia's service. He designs war machines and draws maps.

1503
Pope Alexander VI dies, and Cesare Borgia falls from power. A new pope, Julius II, is elected.

Battle of the Giants

In 1503 Pope Alexander VI died, and his son Cesare Borgia fell from power. Leonardo returned to Florence. He was now a highly regarded artist and was in demand. In autumn of that year, he was commissioned to paint an important fresco—a job that brought him face to face with a rival artist.

In 1494 Florence had become a republic following the expulsion of the ruling Medici family. The city's new authorities wanted to celebrate their successes with huge frescoes in the city hall, the Palazzo della Signoria. They planned to have two frescoes painted on opposite walls inside the council meeting room. Both were to show battles won by Florence against rival Italian cities. One was the Battle of Anghiari (against Milan, 1440) and the other was the Battle of Cascina (against Pisa, 1364). They were major public commissions, and only the greatest artists in Florence were considered. Leonardo was commissioned to paint the Battle of Anghiari, and the artist Michelangelo was commissioned for the Battle of Cascina.

Left: Even though Leonardo's fresco was later painted over, we know what the completed portion of "The Battle of Anghiari" looked like because other artists copied it. This copy of the central part shows the moment when the two sides fought for possession of a flag. It was painted by the Flemish artist Peter Paul Rubens in the early 1600s after he saw an illustration of Leonardo's work.

Spring 1503
Leonardo returns to Florence. He begins work on the "Mona Lisa," his most famous painting.

Autumn 1503
Leonardo starts "The Battle of Anghiari," which he does not finish.

Michelangelo

His full name was Michelangelo di Lodovico Buonarroti (1475–1564) and he was a great Renaissance sculptor, painter, and poet. It took him four years to paint his frescoes on the ceiling of the Sistine Chapel in Rome. Another of his famous works is the marble statue of David. Leonardo saw it and sketched it in one of his notebooks. He was also involved in finding a place to display it in Florence.

Leonardo was 51; Michelangelo was 29. Although they respected each other's work, they were not on friendly terms and had exchanged cross words in public.

Leonardo began by sketching details for the fresco in his notebooks, which he then transferred to a life-size cartoon. It was massive, measuring 60 ft (18 m) wide and 24 ft (7.3 m) high. It took more than a year for Leonardo and his assistants to complete the cartoon, but by June 1505 he was ready to start painting.

He did not use the traditional method of fresco painting, but tried a new technique, using a mixture of oil and tempera paints. The result was a disaster: the plaster did not dry and the oil paints dripped. After 11 months he stopped work, but the portion he did complete was praised for its mastery of human anatomy. Michelangelo gave up on his fresco, too. He did the cartoon for it, then was ordered to Rome to work for Pope Julius II. In the 1560s both frescoes were painted over by Giorgio Vasari.

Right: One of the many drawings by Leonardo for "The Battle of Anghiari." This chalk drawing shows the head of a soldier.

July 9, 1504
Leonardo's father, Ser Piero, dies.

1504
Michelangelo's famous statue of David is unveiled in Florence.

The "Mona Lisa"

Leonardo probably began work on the "Mona Lisa" in 1503. Today the painting can be seen in the Louvre museum in Paris. The woman in the portrait is widely believed to be Lisa Gherardini, wife of Francesco del Giocondo, a Florence silk merchant. Francesco probably commissioned the portrait from Leonardo. The lady would have been addressed as "Monna" Lisa, Monna being short for Madonna, meaning "my lady." Over the years, the English spelling has changed to Mona. In many ways the "Mona Lisa" is a revolutionary painting. Leonardo made full use of the three-quarter pose. He showed her from the waist up and included her hands, and he painted her eyes looking straight at the viewer, not into the distance—a very new idea.

Left: Always a slow painter, Leonardo spent about four years on the "Mona Lisa." He used oil paints, building them up one layer at a time, each time having to wait for the paint to dry before carrying on. He used very fine brushes—so fine that not a single brushstroke can be seen. Leonardo was a perfectionist who took his time. In fact, he never considered he'd finished it, and he kept working on it for the rest of his life. The painting is famous for the strange expression on the lady's face—a half-smile plays about her mouth as if she were caught up in her own private joke.

LOST...

On August 21, 1911, Vincenzo Peruggia, an Italian painter-decorator who worked at the Louvre, removed the "Mona Lisa" from its frame, hid it under his coat, and left the building. The Louvre stayed closed for a week. The theft made headline news (seen here in a newspaper cartoon), songs were written, and even a short film was made about it.

...AND FOUND!

The "Mona Lisa" was missing for two years, until Peruggia tried to sell it to an antiques dealer in Florence. Peruggia said that he wanted the painting to be returned to Italy, where it belonged. His plan backfired, however. The picture was recovered and sent back to the Louvre. Peruggia was imprisoned for 18 months.

The Human Body

Leonardo learned about the world by looking at it in detail. For him, seeing was believing. He did not rely on the work of others, but preferred to investigate things for himself. In all his studies, nowhere is this clearer than in his work on the human body.

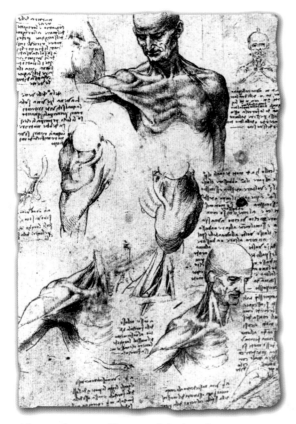

Above: A page of Leonardo's drawings, showing the muscles of the arm and shoulder.

His interest in the structure of the human body began in the 1480s but reached a peak in the early 1500s. Leonardo wanted to know how the body's muscles, bones, and organs worked, and what they looked like. The only way he could do this was by dissection—cutting open dead bodies. By his own count, he dissected the bodies of more than 30 men and women of all ages.

Leonardo wanted to know what the bones of the skeleton looked like, how they were connected, and how they moved. He wanted to understand the muscles that covered the body.

1506
Leonardo returns to Milan with Salai. He is invited by the French governor of the city, Charles d'Amboise.

1507
King Louis XII of France appoints Leonardo his court artist, based in Milan. He meets Francesco Melzi.

> *"The muscles which move the lips of the mouth are more numerous in man than in any other animal; and this is necessary for him on account of the many actions in which these lips are continually employed, as in... whistling, laughing, weeping, and similar actions. Also in the strange contortions used by clowns when they imitate faces."*
>
> **Leonardo da Vinci, *Notebooks***

He wanted to know how the lungs worked, how the eyes could see, and how blood moved through veins. Understanding the body in this way helped him to appreciate it, and this unique knowledge helped him to make his paintings look so lifelike.

Dissection was illegal, so Leonardo had to do it secretly, usually at night. It was messy work, and dangerous, too, as he ran the risk of catching infections from the corpses. After locating the body part he wanted to examine, he washed it, and then drew it. There were times when he needed to repeat the same dissection on two or three bodies, as decay had set in before he had finished his drawing. In total, Leonardo produced around 200 drawings of the human body. Many artists, including Michelangelo, dissected bodies, but Leonardo was the first to see the drawings as an end in themselves rather than as a study for a particular painting.

As he continued his investigations, Leonardo hoped to solve what he called the "great mystery." He wanted to discover the very meaning of human life itself. He wanted to uncover the soul, but he came to realize that this was an impossible quest.

1508

Pope Julius II commissions Michelangelo to decorate the ceiling of the Sistine Chapel in the Vatican.

1509

Leonardo continues his studies of human anatomy.

An Invitation to France

In 1506 Leonardo and Salai returned to Milan. The city was still under French control, and it was the French for whom Leonardo worked during his final years.

In Milan, Charles d'Amboise, the city's French governor, invited Leonardo to design a villa and garden. Leonardo sketched house designs and planned a garden with a mill that pumped water and made instruments play music. It was a grand design, but the villa was never built.

In 1507 King Louis XII of France asked Leonardo to work in Milan as his court artist. Leonardo was paid a salary and designed stage sets for plays.

Then, in 1512, Milan was occupied by an army from Switzerland, the French moved out, the Sforza family returned to power, and Leonardo went to stay with a new friend, a 20-year-old noble named Francesco Melzi.

Left: The chateau of Cloux in France today. The building has been enlarged since Leonardo lived there in the early 1500s.

1512
The French are defeated and leave Milan. Leonardo goes to live with Francesco Melzi.

1513–16
Leonardo divides his time between Florence and Rome. He draws a self-portrait, showing him in his 60s.

Left: According to Giorgio Vasari, Leonardo died in the arms of King François I. This painting, made in 1818 by the French artist Ingres, shows that moment. However, the story is not true. The king was actually elsewhere at the time.

From 1513 to 1516, Leonardo and his companions Salai and Melzi divided their time between Florence and Rome. It was around this time that Leonardo drew his famous self-portrait (see page 45). It shows him in his 60s, with half-closed eyes, as if squinting. In his notebooks he mentions wearing spectacles, so perhaps his eyesight was beginning to fail.

In old age, Leonardo struggled to find a patron in Italy. When the new king of France, François I, made him his official painter in 1516, Leonardo had little reason to stay in Italy. He set off with Melzi, Salai, and mules carrying his pictures and notebooks. They traveled to their new home at Cloux in central France.

At Cloux, Leonardo began putting his notebooks in order, and King François asked him to design a palace. He never completed either of these tasks. On May 2, 1519, at the age of 67, Leonardo died. He was buried at the church of St.-Florentin in Amboise, near Cloux.

Lost grave

The church of St.-Florentin was demolished in 1802, and its graveyard was leveled. It was at this time that the location of Leonardo's final resting place disappeared without a trace. Attempts were later made to find his grave, and some bones were dug up—but no one knows for sure if they are Leonardo's.

Around 1515
Leonardo paints "St. John the Baptist" (see page 3).

1516
Leonardo moves to Cloux, France, to work for King François I as his official painter.

Leonardo's Legacy

Leonardo left the world with a truly remarkable legacy. As we look at his paintings and his notebooks, we travel back in time more than 500 years to Renaissance Italy. There we discover a unique man with a hunger for knowledge, a man whose dreams and discoveries transported him far into the future, a man who was ahead of his time.

Above: A present-day Italian one-euro coin, with one of Leonardo's drawings pictured on the back. The sketch shows how Leonardo studied and planned out the proportions of the human body.

A list of Leonardo's surviving works reads like this: seven paintings done with others, 13 paintings done by himself, about 4,000 drawings, and about 7,000 notebook pages. It is hard to say how much other work has been lost. One painting, "The Battle of Anghiari," may still exist, hidden beneath a later work. Another, "Leda and the Swan," was destroyed in a fire, and maybe as many as 13,000 notebook pages are missing. Despite the losses over the centuries, enough survives for us to appreciate the genius of Leonardo da Vinci.

While he was alive, people praised Leonardo for his musical abilities (he sang and played the lyre) and for his inventions, though few were ever built. Even though he left many paintings unfinished, those that he did complete were renowned for their beauty and perfection.

May 2, 1519
Leonardo dies at Cloux, France, age 67. He is buried in the Church of St.-Florentin in Amboise.

1999
A bronze horse, built to Leonardo's design for the Sforza Monument, is completed.

It is only in the modern era, however, that Leonardo's extraordinary character and greatness have been truly appreciated. In the 1800s researchers started reading his notebooks. Only then could the full picture of this great man emerge—and he took his place as a leading figure in the history of the Renaissance.

We can now see that Leonardo was unmatched by any other living person for centuries. As an artist, he created pictures that have become known all over the world. As an engineer, he designed machines that we recognize today, such as the helicopter, the armored vehicle, and the parachute. And his studies of human anatomy were not bettered for hundreds of years. He was well-rounded, with skills in many different areas, from art to architecture, human anatomy to warfare, science to invention. He is known as a true "Renaissance man."

Below: In 1503 Leonardo drew plans for a bridge at Constantinople (Istanbul, Turkey) that was never built. In 2001 a pedestrian bridge, built to Leonardo's design, was opened at Aas, Norway. It proves that his graceful design actually worked.

2001

A bridge built to Leonardo's design is opened in Norway.

2002

Leonardo's sketch of the proportions of the human body is put on the back of Italy's new one-euro coin.

Glossary

alliance a formal agreement between two or more countries, cities, or states, usually for a military purpose.

altarpiece a religious painting that sits at the back of a church altar.

anatomy the study of the shape and structure of a plant or animal, especially of the human body.

Annunciation the announcement by the angel Gabriel to Mary that she will give birth to Jesus.

apprentice a person who enters into an agreement with an artist or craftsperson to work for him for a set period of time. In return, the apprentice is taught the basics of the art or craft.

cartoon from the Italian word *cartone*, meaning a big sheet of paper. In Renaissance art, a cartoon was a detailed working drawing that was made for a fresco; it was usually drawn the same size as the finished work.

chapel a small place of Christian worship that is usually attached to a larger building, such as a cathedral, monastery, fortress, or castle.

circa meaning approximately or around; often abbreviated as "c."

commission to employ an artist, builder, or craftsperson to create something. In Leonardo's day, commissions were handed out by wealthy people called patrons.

dissection the process of carefully cutting open a plant or animal in order to examine its internal structure.

dredger a large boat fitted with scoops that are used to dig out the bottom of a river or a canal and keep it clear.

fortifications structures that are designed to protect a town or building from attack.

fresco a picture painted onto a wall while the plaster is still damp. As the plaster dries, the paint binds to the plaster, and the image becomes part of the wall.

genius a person who has exceptional intelligence, creativity, or natural ability.

guild a group of people who belong to the same craft, trade, or profession and who band together to protect their common interests.

illegitimate a child born to parents who are not married to each other.

lyre a U-shaped musical instrument with strings.

Magi according to the Bible, three wise men from the East who brought gifts to the infant Jesus.

marquetry a craft using thin pieces of different colored woods to make patterns and pictures.

Middle Ages a period in history from about the 5th century to the 14th century.

mold a shape or frame around which a material can be shaped.

mineral a substance that is formed naturally, such as a rock or crystal.

Nativity the birth of Christ, or a painting or sculpture of that subject.

oil paint a paint that is made by mixing powdered pigments (colors) in plant oil.

Ottoman Empire a Turkish empire in Europe, Asia, and Africa which lasted from the 13th century until the early 20th century.

panel painting a painting made on a solid material such as a piece of wood. Poplar was the favorite wood of Renaissance artists, but walnut and pear wood were also used.

passport an official document that allows a person to travel freely between different territories or countries.

patron a person who pays an artist.

perspective a method of showing three-dimensional distance in a two-dimensional painting or drawing, using techniques such as making more distant objects in the scene look smaller than those that are closer.

pigment a substance that adds color. In Leonardo's time, the colors for paints came from naturally occurring elements, such as tin, which was used to make white.

pope the head of the Roman Catholic Church. Today, the pope's official residence is the Vatican City, which is surrounded by the city of Rome, Italy.

portrait a picture that shows the likeness of an individual.

proficient fully skilled.

Renaissance from a French word meaning "rebirth." It was a movement in art, literature, and science in which the cultures of ancient Greece and Rome were rediscovered, leading to a rebirth of culture in Europe. It involved developments such as greater realism in painting. It began in 14th-century Italy and spread through Europe.

Renaissance man a man who is highly skilled in several different fields of study, particularly in both arts and sciences. The ability to master several fields was an ideal of the Renaissance period.

republic a country or city-state in which power is in the hands of the people and their elected representatives.

tempera a method of painting with ground-up powdered pigments mixed with water and fresh egg yolk. It was used in Europe between the 12th and 15th centuries.

three-quarter view a type of view where the object faces slightly to one side and is neither straight on or sideways; used particularly in reference to portraits.

varnish a clear liquid that dries to form a hard protective layer on the surface of a picture or piece of furniture.

vellum a type of smooth writing paper made from calfskin.

villa a large house in the country.

volatile prone to sudden tempers.

workshop a room or building where things are made. An artist's workshop produced works of art commissioned by patrons.

Bibliography

Bramly, Serge, *Leonardo: The Artist and the Man*, Penguin, London, 1994

Kemp, Martin, *Leonardo*, Taschen, Köln, 2000

Nicholl, Charles, *Leonardo da Vinci: The Flights of the Mind*, Allen Lane, London, 2004

Sassoon, Donald, *Mona Lisa: The History of the World's Most Famous Painting*, HarperCollins, London, 2001

Vasari, Giorgio, translated by George Bull, *Lives of the Artists*, Penguin, London, 1965

Zöllner, Frank, *Leonardo*, Oxford University Press, Oxford, 2004

Sources of quotes:

p. 13 *Lives of the Artists*, Giorgio Vasari, Penguin, London, 1965

pp. 21, 34, 49, 55 *The Notebooks of Leonardo da Vinci*, Irma A. Richter, Oxford University Press, Oxford, 1952

Some Web sites that will help you explore Leonardo's world:

www.mos.org/leonardo
A showcase of Leonardo's life and work.

www.leonet.it/comuni/vinci
Official Web site of the Leonardo Museum, located in Vinci, Italy, where Leonardo was born.

www.bbc.co.uk/science/leonardo
An interactive journey through Leonardo's life and works to discover what made him a Renaissance man.

www.lairweb.org.nz/leonardo/index.html
Detailed information about Leonardo, with a good selection of images of his paintings, drawings, and inventions.

Index

Acknowledgments

B = bottom, C = center, T = top, L = left, R = right.

Front cover Corbis/Alinari Archives; **1** The Bridgeman Art Library/The Louvre, Paris; **3** Scala Archives/ The Louvre, Paris; **7–8** Scala Archives/Uffizi, Florence; **10** Scala Archives/Castello del Buonconsiglio, Trento; **12** The Art Archive/San Agostino, San Gimignano; **14T** Scala Archives, Florence/The Louvre, Paris; **14B** Scala Archives/Uffizi, Florence; **15T** The Bridgeman Art Library/National Gallery, London; **15B** AKG-images/Museum Czartoryski, Cracow; **16** The Bridgeman Art Library/Museo de Firenze Com'era; **17** The Bridgeman Art Library/Bargello, Florence; **19** The Bridgeman Art Library/Uffizi; **20** Corbis/National Gallery, London; **22** Scala Archives/State Archives, Florence; **23** AKG-images/National Gallery of Art, Washington; **24** Scala Archives/Museo di San Marco, Florence; **25** The Bridgeman Art Library/Vatican Museums and Galleries; **26–27** Scala Archives/Palazzo Medici-Riccardi, Florence; **27** Corbis/Ted Speigel; **28** The Bridgeman Art Library/Uffizi, Florence; **29** Scala Archives/Uffizi, Florence; **31** AKG-images/Santa Maria delle Grazie, Milan; **32** The Royal Collection © 2005, Her Majesty Queen Elizabeth II; **35** AKG-images/Rabatti-Domingie/Gabinetto Disegnie Stampe, Florence; **36** Art Archive/ Biblioteca Nacional, Madrid/Joseph Martin; **37T** Corbis/James L Amos; **37C** The Bridgeman Art Library/ Bibliotheque de l'Institut de France, Paris; **37B** Corbis/Seth Joel; **38** The Bridgeman Art Library/ Bibliotheque de l'Institut de France, Paris; **40** AKG-images/Biblotheque de l'Institut de France, Paris; **41** Scala Archives, Florence/Museo della Scienza e della Technica, Milan; **42** AKG-images/Santa Maria delle Grazie, Milan; **45** Corbis/Alinari Archives; **46** Scala Archives, Florence/Museo Vinciano, Vinci; **47** Corbis/ National Gallery Collection by kind permission of the Trustees of the National Gallery, London; **48** AKG-images/British Museum, London; **49** The Art Archive/Dagli Orti; **50** AKG-images/Ackademie de Bildenden Kunste, Vienna; **51** AKG-images/Szepmuveszeti Museum, Budapest; **52** The Bridgeman Art Library/ Louvre, Paris/Giraudon; **53** Rex Features/Roger-Viollet; **54** Corbis/Bettmann; **56** Corbis/Brian Harding, Eye Ubiquitous; **57** AKG-images/Musee du Petit Palais, Paris; **58** Marshall Editions Archives; **59** Terje Johansen, Studio S/International Projects Liaison Leonardo Bridge Project/Brickfish Creative.